MORE

Jokes

for

the

John

"MORE Jokes For The John" is a soul-mate to "Poems For The John", "Jokes For The John", "Guest Register For The John" and "Flushed". They are our John series, considered the greatest bathroom advance since the invention of the doorlock.

We wish to credit the following people who contributed to the success of this new movement (and without whose assistance this book would have been written anyway):

Ophilia Keester	Corn Cob, Ill.
Sophia Plopp	Oo-ah, N.Y.
Stanley Upclose	Urinal, Calif.
I. P. Standing	Virgin Stream, Maryland
S. Catology	Cesspool, Idaho

A maiden aunt is a **girl** who never had sense enough to say 'uncle.'

"But Fred, are you **sure** this is what they mean by the 'Rhythm Method'?"

It was the nurse's day off and the doctor stuck his head into the waiting room to ask, "Who's next?" each time a patient left. One guy got up and said, "Me, doc." "What's your trouble," asked the doctor. So the guy told him!!!

The doctor grabbed him by the arm, pulled him into his office and bawled him out. "Never do that again! Especially not in a roomful of people! Next time, just say that your nose or your eyes bother you." A couple of weeks went by and the fellow came back. The nurse was off again and when the doctor asked, "Who's next?" the same guy said, "I am."

The doctor asked, "What's your trouble?" The guy replied, "My ear's bothering me." "What's wrong with it?" "I can't urinate out of it!"

The shapely young nurse was walking down the hospital corridor with her uniform askew and part of her bosom showing when she encountered her supervisor. The supervisor bawled her out for improper dress and shameful display of her body. Straightening her clothes in confusion, the young nurse blurted the excuse, "I'm terribly sorry but you know those damn interns never put anything away!"

"I'm not running this place for your entertainment, Bernice. Let's get this show on the bed, eh."

There was once a Broadway playboy who had the reputation of winding up under the table every time he went to a night club with a pretty girl. Not drunk, you understand . . . just an insatiable curiosity.

"Of course I'm nervous! I'm always nervous the first time."

While hunting, the man saw a beautiful nude woman come running out of the woods and disappear across the clearing. As she got out of sight, three men dressed in white uniforms came running out of the same woods. "Hey, you," yelled one of them, "did you see a woman come by here?"

"Yes," replied the hunter. "What's the trouble?"

"She's an inmate of the Happy Hollow asylum, and gets loose every now and then. We're trying to catch her."

"I can understand that," said the hunter, "But why is one of you carrying a bucket of sand in his hand?"

"He caught her last time," said the spokesman, "that's his handicap."

Roger Poontang was in an expansive mood, so he called his girl friend and invited her to dinner. They felt like eating Chinese food and decided to go to the famous House of Hunglo. When ordering, Roger thought he'd have a little fun, and said to the waiter:

"Bling me some flied lice."

The waiter left and returned with Won Ton soup. They ate it, and Roger again said to the waiter:

"We want flied lice."

This time the waiter brought them two orders of egg roll. As the waiter walked away, Roger called loud enough for everyone in the restaurant to hear:

"How about that flied lice!"

At that, the Chinese waiter halted, walked back, leaned toward Roger and said:

"Can't you pronounce fried rice — you plick?"

"Goodness! This is all so new to me—what do we do next?"

The owner of a large furniture store in the mid-west arrived in New York on a buying trip. As he was checking in to the hotel he struck up an acquaintance with a beautiful young lady. However, she was French and they couldn't understand a word of each other's language.

He took out a pencil and notebook and drew a picture of a taxi. She smiled, nodded her head and they went for a ride in the park.

Later, he drew a picture of a table in a restaurant with a question mark and she nodded, so they went to dinner.

After dinner he sketched two dancers and she was delighted. They went to several night clubs, drank champagne, danced and had a glorious evening. It had gotten quite late when she motioned for the pencil and drew a picture of a four-poster bed. He was dumbfounded, and has never been able to understand how she knew he was in the furniture business.

He spent $3,000.00 on a halitosis cure and found out that no one liked him anyway.

She was a calendar model, 'til she skipped a couple of months.

The cause of many divorces is the old tale!''—

Two ancient salesmen were discussing their former exploits on the road. One said to the other, "I don't think there's as much sex, romance and love going on as there used to be." "Sure there is," said the second. "Only there's a new crowd doing it!"

"So what if you **do** always lose. Look at the nice consolation prize you get."

"Hey, your wife is goodlooking, isn't she?"
"Yes, I think she's rather attractive."
"She's a lot of fun too, isn't she?"
"Yeah, we have a lot of laughs together."
"Really built, huh?"
"Are you kiddin'. Monroe's got nothing on her!"
"So how come you're trying to make **my** wife?"

This is National Be Kind To Sex Offender Week, so when a committee worker comes to your door, attack her.

"I don't care what they told you when you started here. I'm **not** one of the fringe benefits."

Sirs Hardwicke and Cedric, the notorious big African game hunters, were lunching at their posh London club. The waitress was hovering nearby.

"Hardy, old chap," harumphed Cedric, "I do believe the word is spelled 'w-o-o-m-b'."

"No, Ceddie, old bean," answered Sir Hardwicke, "I'm really quite sure it is spelled 'w-o-o-o-m-b'."

"Begging your pardon, sirs," said the waitress, who had overheard the conversation, "but I believe the word you are seeking is spelled 'w-o-m-b'."

Turning to Sir Cedric, Sir Hardwicke said, "I say, old man, it is quite plain that this young lady has never heard a large elephant relieve himself!"

Mr. and Mrs. Frisbie had so many quarrels after they retired nights that they finally decided to have separate rooms. This worked out very nicely for a few nights, but one evening before retiring, Mrs. Frisbie coyly remarked, "Jonathan, if you ever get lonesome for me during the night and feel that you need me, just step into the hall and whistle."

A few nights later, Jonathan was just getting to sleep when he heard his wife's voice softly saying over the transom:

"Jonathan dear, did I hear you whistle?"

"Well, I'm glad you finally got home, Bagstone. I was just discussing with the little woman here, some of the **really big** plans I have for your future down at the office."

Hey Pop: "What's a Lesbian?"
Pop: "Ask Mom, he'll tell you."

A man went to visit his favorite lady of the night. He rang the bell and found there was no answer. Then, he put on his glasses and read a note that was pinned to the door: ON VACATION. DO IT YOURSELF.

"Now, remember; don't try to make every man you meet—just my boss."

The neighborhood's most notorious tippler, making his way unsteadily homeward, encountered the parish priest who inquired about the suspicious bulge in his coat pocket.

"It's holy water, Father," the culprit protested piously.

The priest removed the bottle, sniffed at it and announced that it contained whiskey.

"Glory be," cried the drunk. "A miracle!"

"Why darling...what ever makes you think that I've been out with another man?"

The young husband, a do-it-yourselfer, decided that his bathroom fixtures needed a new coat of paint. He applied the first coat to the toilet seat and went down to the basement to get a new brush. Meanwhile, his wife, feeling nature's call, sat on the seat and completed her assignment. To her horror, she found herself stuck to the seat. Upon hearing his wife's shrieks, the husband rushed up from the basement and tried to pull her loose, but to no avail. In desperation, he unscrewed the entire toilet seat, carried the seat and his wife into the bedroom and ran to the phone to call the doctor. When the doctor arrived, the husband said, "Come into the bedroom. I want to show you something you'll never believe." He pulled back the sheet, exposing his wife and said to the doctor, "What do you think?"

The doctor replied, "I think it's lovely but why frame it!"

A toast of wine to Dianna devine,
To her eyes, her hair, her beauty so rare,
To her rosebud lips that smile so serene,
To her lovely full hips, her fingertips,
Her languid arms, her devastating charms . . .
And those several parts I have not seen.

"You're a little late—You'll have to be satisfied with seconds."

The old man stood at the gates of the cemetery and wept. A passer-by stopped to comfort him.

"Why are you crying?" the latter asked softly.

"My daughter is laying in there," explained the weeping one. "Sometimes I wish she was dead."

The teacher was unable to tolerate the conduct of little Jackie any longer and finally sent him home with a note requesting his mother to come see her before Jackie returned to class.

When the mother arrived, the teacher said: "That son of yours is completely unmanageable and will not obey."

"Yes, I know," answered the mother. "He's just like his father."

"He curses," continued the teacher, "and he is continually molesting and pinching little girls."

"Just like his father," repeated the mother.

"But not only that, he steals from the other children," the teacher went on, "and if they complain, he beats them."

"Just like his father," the mother said again. "I'm sure glad I didn't marry that man!"

"Interested in learning how to save yourself $3,458, Mister?"

Once upon a time there was a beautiful young girl taking a stroll through the woods. All at once she saw an extremely ugly bull frog seated on a log and to her amazement the bull frog spoke to her.

"Maiden," croaked the frog, "would you do me a big favor? This will be hard for you to believe, but I was once a handsome, charming prince and then a mean, ugly, old witch cast a spell over me and turned me into a frog."

"Oh, what a pity!" exclaimed the pretty girl. "I'll do anything I can to help you break such a spell."

"Well, Miss," replied the frog, "the only way that this spell can be taken off and I can be returned to a handsome young man again is for some lovely and pretty young girl to take me home and let me spend the night under her pillow."

The young girl took the ugly frog home and placed him beneath her pillow that night when she retired. When she awoke the next morning, sure enough, there beside her in the bed was a very young, handsome man, and plainly of royal blood.

And so they lived happily ever after, except that until this day her father and mother still do not believe her story.

Marriage is the process of finding out what kind of guy your wife would have preferred.

"Now **cut** that out!"

Sam went to his psychiatrist complaining of a hatred for elephants. "I can't stand elephants," he explained. "I lay awake nights despising them. The thought of an elephant fills me with loathing."

"Sam," said the psychiatrist, "there's only one thing for you to do. Go to Africa, organize a safari, find an elephant in the jungle and shoot it. That way you'll get it out of your system."

Sam immediately made arrangements for a safari hunt in Africa, inviting his best friend to join him. They arrived in Nairobi and lost no time getting out on the jungle trails. After they had been hunting for sev-

Continued

eral days, Sam's best friend grabbed him by the arm one morning and yelled at him:

"Sam, Sam, Sam! Over there behind that tree there's an elephant! Sam Get your gun—no, no, not **that** gun—the rifle with the long barrel! Now aim it! QUICK! SAM! QUICK! No! Not that way—this way! Be sure you don't pull the trigger till he moves a little to the right! WAIT SAM! Don't let the elephant see you! Be sure to aim at his head!"

Sam whirled around, took aim, and shot and killed his friend. He was put in prison and his psychiatrist flew to Africa to visit him.

"I sent you over here to shoot an elephant and instead you shoot your best friend," the psychiatrist said. "Why?"

"Well," Sam replied, "there's only one thing in the world that I hate more than an elephant and that is a loudmouth know-it-all!"

A woman walked into a very busy butcher shop. Looking at the meats and poultry on display, she suddenly grabbed hold of a dressed chicken. She picked up one wing, sniffed it; picked up the other wing, sniffed it; picked up one leg, sniffed it; picked up the other leg, sniffed it. Just as she finished sniffing the second leg, the butcher walked up to her and said, "Madam, could **you** pass such a test?"

A young honeymoon couple were touring southern Florida and happened to stop at one of the rattlesnake farms along the road. After seeing the sights, they engaged in small talk with the man that handled the snakes.

"Gosh!" exclaimed the new bride. "You certainly have a dangerous job. Don't you ever get bitten by the snakes?"

"Yes, I do," answered the handler.

"Well," she insisted, "just what do you do when you are bitten by a snake?"

"I always carry a razor-sharp knife in my pocket, and as soon as I am bitten, I make deep criss-cross marks across the fang wounds and then suck the poison from the wound."

"What, uh . . . what would happen if you were to accidentally sit on a rattler?" persisted the bride.

"Ma'am," answered the snake handler, "that will be the day I learn who my real friends are."

"Did I hear a zipper?"

"She works for the U. N. and can say **yes** in twenty-four languages."

Two fellows, who had studied economics at college, upon graduation formed a partnership and opened a store. It failed in three months. A guy who had no schooling bought the place from them and made a huge success of it.

The former partners had occasion to talk to him. "Look, we studied economic science and failed in business. You bought the store from us and made a good go of it...how do you explain it?"

"Well, I'll tell you," answered the unlearned guy. "I'm a plain, simple business man. I buy a thing for a dollar and resell it for two dollars... I'm satisfied with my one per cent profit!"

Texan in tailor shop viewing his new suit in a three way mirror. The tailor asked, "Well what do you think?" "Great," the Texan replied, "I'll take all three of 'em."

"I certainly do intend to make things right —you'll always have a job in my office."

She had her suspicions for a long time, but when he arrived home late one night with signs of lipstick on his cheek, she decided it was time to speak.

"Now look here, Reggie," she complained, "I'll have you know once and for all that I will not play second fiddle!"

"Sec'n fiddle!" he shrieked, "Sec'n fiddle! You can take it from me, Evelyn, you're damn lucky to be in the ruddy band at all!"

The young sailor had missed his ship. As he watched it steaming majestically under the Golden Gate Bridge he clasped his arms a little tighter around the girl's waist and with a sad look on his face he mumbled: "Now, honey, we're both in trouble."

"Are you married?"

Diane lay sprawled in sweet exhaustion on the bed, her attire consisting of one earring. Beside her, Bob wore a full length coat of tan. He slowly lit two cigarettes and passed one to Diane. For a long moment, smoke and silence hung in the air, then: "My mother always told me to be good," Diane said with a little smile. "Was I?"

He had been bitten by a dog, but didn't give it much thought until he noticed that the wound was taking a remarkably long time to heal. Finally he consulted a doctor who took one look at it and ordered the dog brought in. Just as he had suspected, the dog had rabies. Since it was too late to give the patient serum, the doctor felt he had to prepare him for the worst. The poor man sat down at the doctor's desk and began to write. His physician tried to comfort him.

"Perhaps it won't be so bad," he said. "You needn't make out your will right now."

"I'm not making any will," replied the man. "I'm just writing out a list of people I'm going to bite!"

"My doctor says I'll have to see you only once a month, you're too many calories!"

"If exercise eliminates fat, how come women get double chins?"

Henry and Irving were business partners and one day Henry went to New York City to purchase some furnishings for their new office. The furniture proprietor convinced Henry to buy a magic lamp. Henry rubbed the lamp and the Genie appeared and promised to grant him three wishes. Henry immediately wished for a million dollars. A few minutes later, Irving phoned the store and said: "Henry! The greatest thing just happened. Two million dollars just now fell on my desk!"

Again Henry made a wish. This time it was for a beautiful red-head and again Irving called, "Henry, you'd never believe it, but two gorgeous red-heads just dropped into my office!"

It was then that the Genie appeared and explained to Henry that anything he wished for his partner would receive double. Henry thought a moment and irritated at having to do all of the work while his partner was getting twice the benefits, decided on his next wish. However, before asking it he called his doctor and asked: "Are you sure it doesn't hurt much to have one of them removed?"

MADAME: Mona, just how accomplished are you?

MONA: I don't like to brag, but I can make love standing on my head!

MADAME: Then you're the one I want ...there's a yogi waiting downstairs.

"Just ignore her, Mr. Conway. She's at that age where she's constantly seeking attention."

The wedding date was set and the groom's three pals—a carpenter, an electrician and a dentist—were deciding what pranks to play on the couple on their wedding night.

The carpenter figured sawing the slats of their bed would give them a chuckle or two.

The electrician decided he'd wire the bed —with alternating current of course.

The dentist wouldn't commit himself but wore a sly grin and promised a real lulu. The nuptials came off as planned, and a few days later each of the groom's buddies received the following note:

"DEAR FRIEND,
    WE DIDN'T MIND THE BED SLATS BEING SAWED. THE ELECTRIC SHOCK WAS ONLY A MINOR THING. BUT BY GOD, I'M GONNA KILL THE GUY WHO PUT NOVACAINE IN THE VASELINE!"

A policeman came home late and, undressing in the dark, slipped into bed. His wife awoke and said, "Clancy, would ye mind runnin' down and gettin' me a headache powder? My head's splittin'."

Clancy fumbled into some clothing and went out to the drugstore. The druggist stared at him and said, "By the way, aren't you officer Clancy?" Clancy nodded.

"Well, then," asked the druggist, "what are you doing in that fireman's uniform?"

"Go ahead and shoot, man! Damn it, SHOOT!"

"Mama, Mama, don't wait for the shrimp boats, sister is coming home with the crabs."

"I hope you remembered to leave a call for 7 A.M., Mister. I wouldn't want to be late for school."

A beautiful, young and unmarried movie starlet was throwing a large party in her swanky home for all the men she knew. As the party went on into the wee small hours, the hefty-chested young babe drank more and more liquor, but she resisted the advances of her various bachelor guests.

Finally at about 5:30 A.M. she said goodnight to the last guest and slumped down on the living room couch, dead drunk.

The next morning she found herself in her own bed, clad in her sheerest nightgown. Surprised she went down to breakfast.

"Wang Lee," she asked her Chinese man-servant, as he served the table, "how did I get to my room last night?"

"I put you there, Missy," he answered.

"Gee," she said, "I must have really been on my back."

"First time on back, Missy," he replied. "Second time on side; third time on stairs; fourth time . . ."

Harry's Bar in Paris has a new concoction that is all the rage. It's called M.R.S. Punch. They make it with milk, rum and sugar and it's a gasser. The milk is for vitality and the sugar is for pep. They put in the rum, so people will know what to do with all that pep and vitality.

"You have a beauty of a chest cold."

One of London's "ladies of the evening," picked up an American tourist in Picadilly Circus. She took him to her rooms, promptly undressed and got into bed. He, too, got out of his clothes but left on his shoes. "Come now," she said, "we can't have that. Take off your shoes."
"What," shot back the American, "and maybe catch athlete's foot?"

A young plumber was called to a woman's apartment in New York to repair a leaking pipe. When he arrived he was pleased to discover that the woman was quite a luscious, well-stacked dish and during the course of the afternoon the two became extremely friendly. About 5:30 P.M. the phone rang disturbing the bedroom shenanigans.

"That was my husband," she said, putting down the phone. "He's on his way home but is going back to the office around eight. Come back then, dear, and we can take up where we left off."

The union plumber looked at the woman in disbelief. "What? On my own time??"

"Now comes the hard part...separating the men from the girls!!"

"I thought I heard someone yell 'Ouch'!"

The old gentleman was advised by his doctor that he needed "Mother's milk." He went home and explained the situation to his wife. She, in turn, suggested that he see their next-door neighbor, who had just given birth and had plenty to spare. He went next door and explained his predicament to his neighbor. She, in turn, told him that she would be happy to oblige. She stripped to the waist and he went to work. After ten minutes of this, she became a little excited and looking down at him said, "Is there anything else you want?" He stopped for a moment, looked up and replied, "Maybe you can get me a couple of cookies?"

It was tea-time in the pad, and the air hung heavy in thick, blue folds as the beat bunch and their tourist friends lit up. Suddenly a loud voice in the hall demanded that they open up, "in the name of the Law." The smokers frantically gathered their still-smoldering weeds and stuffed them in the cuckoo clock. The fuzz broke in and searched carefully but couldn't find anything so they left. The bunch heaved a collective sigh of relief and headed for the clock to recover the stuff. At that moment the hand moved to 3:00 A.M. The little door opened; the bird staggered out and cheeped, "Say man, what time is it?"

The statement of the decade was voiced by Christine Jorgenson when she looked at her Doctor on that fateful night in Denmark and said: "Doc, I had a Ball."

He had been a most eligible bachelor, but now he was on his way to get married. As luck would have it, his car was involved in an accident, and a thorough examination revealed only a ligament laceration in a most intimate place. Despite his protestations, the doctor insisted on putting a splint on it, consisting mainly of four small strips of narrow wood bound together.

When the groom and his bride were alone in their boudoir that night she proceeded to disrobe in a most provocative manner. When she unveiled her shoulders she said, "Look, Dear, never been touched by any man."

Then she stripped to the waist and said, "Look, darling, no other man's eyes have ever gazed upon these."

She continued this routine until finally the groom could contain himself no longer. Indicating his damaged organ, he said, "That's nothing. Look at this...still in the original crate!"

A spirited session of poker was in progress as a new arrival, a practical joker, proceeded to spray the nearest player with the contents of a perfume atomizer.

"Hey, don't spray that on me," the player shouted, "my wife will think I spent the evening in a brothel!"

The player sitting next to him said, "You can squirt me if you like. My wife was never in a brothel and she won't recognize the smell."

"Let me speak to the plumber. I've got a leak in my sink."
"Go ahead, it's your sink!"

"How does it feel being the wife of the Flying Frederick?"

A young woman on a rough Atlantic crossing was in her cabin undressing for bed when suddenly she was overcome by seasickness. She rushed into the corridor and headed for the bathroom. It was not until she collided with an elderly gentleman who was feeling equally miserable that she realized she didn't have a stitch of clothing on. Horrified she let out a shriek.

Her fellow sufferer looked at her sadly. "Don't let it bother you, miss," he moaned. "I'll never live to tell anyone."

A salesman stopped at a small town hotel and had difficulty getting a room. He was about to leave when the clerk said, "I think I may be able to put you up. There are two beds up in room 10 and one is occupied by a woman. But there's a screen around her bed and she's sleeping soundly. Just go to your bed quietly and everything will be fine."

The offer was quickly accepted. About twenty minutes later the salesman returned greatly excited.

"Good heavens," he cried. "The woman in that other bed is dead."

"I know that," said the clerk. "But how the hell did you find out?"

"Man! Where d'you buy your calendars?"

Two gals were chatting on the street corner when a third went riding by in a new compact car.

"I understand," meowed one of the cats, "that she did it for a lark."

"You'd better pick someone else. You can't really enjoy her if you're double-parked."

A young couple about to be married were shopping for a house in the country and after satisfying themselves that they'd found a likely spot, drove back to town. A short time later, however, the girl realized that their new home had no "water closet," or at least they hadn't noticed one.

They wrote their landlord asking where that most necessary of conveniences was located, but shyly referred to the water closet as a "W.C."

Of course Pinch-penny Perry didn't have the foggiest notion what a "W.C." was, but he asked some

Continued

friends who responded with this dilly: "W.C." stood for Wesleyan Church! The landlord thus wrote this letter:

In reply to your letter, the "W.C." is situated about nine miles from your house. I'll admit the distance appears to be great but if you're in the habit of going regularly you'll be glad to know a large number of people take their lunch along and make a day of it. Others who don't have cars take chartered buses which arrive just in time. The last time my wife and I went was six years ago, and attendance was so good we had to stand. Of course it pains me not to be able to go more often. It's really a charming place with a seating capacity of 300 and standing room for 50 more. It may also interest you to know that a bazaar is going to be held to raise funds for furnishing the "W.C." with plush seats, a long-felt need.

Respectfully yours,
Perry Pinkham."

She: "Darling, if I marry you I'll lose my job."
He: "But can't we keep the marriage a secret?"
She: "But suppose we have a baby?"
He: "Oh, we'll tell the baby, of course."

Many a fellow who thinks he's going on a maiden voyage with a girl finds out later it was just a shake-down cruise.

"You'd do well to pattern yourself after Gimble, Rogers. He seems to manage quite well on the $37.50 we pay **him** as a Teller."

Now that Mrs. Newrich was in the money, she had to have the same or better than her neighbors in the way of furnishings. She went to the city's leading antique store and in her ritziest manner commanded: "I want to see some period furniture!" The clerk bowed humbly and asked, "Do you wish to see period examples of Early American, Old English or French Empire?"

"No," she replied, "I want the kind that when the neighbors see it, they should drop dead—PERIOD!"

Business men often wonder how their office telephones are answered for them in their absence. This happened at a swank Madison Avenue Advertising Agency to a top executive. One day his sister-in-law phoned him and was informed by a sweet, young voice that Mr. A. was away from his desk. The sister-in-law then asked if he would be away very long. "No. I don't think so," said the secretary, "he didn't take the newspaper with him."

"Looks like he went to the corner newsstand to get your paper one time too many!"

Underdeveloped young Joe,
Told his gal, nymphomaniac Flo,
"I do like to sport . . .
But let's cut this thing short . . .
'Cause this is as far as I go."

Gently massaging the trick knee of his beautiful, curvaceous patient, the doctor inquired:
"What's a joint like this doing in a nice girl like you?"

"I never wear my wedding ring when I go to an obstetrician. You should hear some of the lectures I get..."

At the wedding between two bop musicians, the preacher read the marriage contract, then asked the couple, "Do you dig this bit?" Both nodded, and the minister proceeded with the ceremony, asking the bride, "Chick, do you dig this cat?" She replied, "Crazy!" He turned to the bridegroom, "Cat, love this chick?" "Mostest," the man answered. The minister then joined their hands and pronounced over them, "Make it, man!"

The new patron was amazed by the extreme cleanliness of the restaurant. A waiter approached the table. "Good afternoon, sir. And what will it be?" he asked. "I'll have the hamburger plate," the patron said.

As the waiter headed for the kitchen, the diner noticed that he wore a spotless white apron and clean white gloves. He marvelled at the immaculate surroundings. Soon the waiter returned, uncovered a casserole dish on the cart to reveal two tempting hamburgers. From a covered pocket in his apron he produced a small pair of shining silver tongs and with them he transferred the meat patties from the steaming casserole to the diner's plate. "We never touch anything with our hands," he explained.

The patron could withold his wonderment no longer. "It's astounding," he found himself saying to the waiter, "how clean everything is here."

The waiter continued serving. "Confidentially," he said, "we even have a special set of rules about visiting the lavatory. Do you see this little piece of string attached to my apron?"

"Yes," the diner answered. "I noticed all the waiters had that and I was wondering what it was for."

The waiter put a large browned potato on the plate with his tongs. "Well," he began, "if I should have to go to the bathroom, that string comes in very handy. I simply unzip my pants and take it out with that piece of string. That way everything stays sanitary."

The patron was puzzled. "But how do you put it back?" he asked.

"I don't know about the other guys," the waiter confided, "but I use these tongs.

PLATONIC FRIENDSHIP is what develops when two people grow tired of making love to each other.

The husband leaned over to his wife and asked, "Come on honey, let's make love."

His wife replied, George, I wish you wouldn't talk that way; the children might hear you. Whenever you're in the mood, why don't you say to me, 'Honey, I'd like to use your washing machine'."

A few nights later, the wife felt in a romantic mood and leaning over to her husband, asked, "George, would you like to use my washing machine?" George replied, "To tell you the truth, dear, it was just a small bundle. I did it by hand."

"I thought your wife didn't approve of your drinking before 5 o'clock, Fenwyck."

Many girls are music lovers. Others can love without it.

"Have you heard the one about the near-sighted turtle that raped an army helmet?"

"I told you this was an authentic costume —complete with chastity belt."

And today's story has a minister alone on the first tee. He sees a fellow standing there and suggests they play together. After a couple of holes, the stranger tells the minister what he's doing wrong. As they play along, the minister gets more advice, all of it good. The man of the cloth finishes the round six strokes under his usual score. He thanks his golf partner and the fellow says: "That will be $75.00. I'm the pro here." The minister argues but to no avail. So he tells the pro to drop over to the rectory that evening to collect his fee. "And when you come," suggests the minister, "bring your mother and father. I'll marry them at the same time!"

The teacher took her class of little boys and girls on an outing, near a race track. As the kids left the bus, several of them had to answer the call of nature.

Naturally, the teacher helped them. She was helping one very cute little fellow when he said: "Please lady, would you mind letting me button my own pants? I'm in a terrible hurry . . . I have to get to the track in time to ride in the third race."

"We don't drink coffee."

The model ascended the ladder
As Titian, the painter, had bade her.
Her position, to Titian,
Suggested coition.
So he climbed up the ladder
and had her.

Inmate: "I have mad insane desire to crush you in my arms."
Lady Psychiatrist: "Now you're talking sense."

"To Sex!"

The family was very disturbed. The patriarch of the clan, Amos, aged 75, decided to get married. What worried his relatives was the fact that the bride Amos selected was a young, healthy, 22 year old. One of Amos's sons button-holed him and pleaded.

"Look, Dad, you must give this more thought. It's very serious. In fact, a thing like this could prove fatal!"

"So what?" answered Amos unperturbedly. "If she dies, I'll marry again."

Joe Lacy had just returned from a month-long trip to New York and he met a good friend just outside his office.

"Joe," said the friend, "what's wrong? I've never seen your eyes so bloodshot!"

"It happened on the trip," said Joe. "My very first evening in New York I met this attractive young woman in a cocktail lounge, and after a night on the town we wound up at my hotel.

"The next morning her crying woke me up. I asked her what was wrong and she told me she was married and that she was now heartily ashamed of herself.

"Well, that started me thinking about my wife and kids back here so before I knew it I was crying along with her."

"But, Joe," said the puzzled friend, "that was almost four weeks ago. What does that have to do with your eyes being bloodshot today?"

"Well, look," Joe explained, "you can't sit and cry your eyes out every morning for four weeks without making them a little red!"

The gentleman walked briskly into the drug store, strode over to the pharmacist and said "I would like a box of Sex-Lax."

The pharmacist smiled and replied, "you must mean Ex-Lax."

"No," the man responded, "I don't have any trouble **going.**"

CRAZY MARRIED COUPLE: She runs after everything that wears pants, and he runs after everything that doesn't.

"Gad! What a waste of **premium** advertising space!!!"

One of the nurses at the state hospital for the insane lured a young male patient into an empty room where she seduced him. Immediately he burst out crying bitterly.

"Here's five dollars. Now stop your crying," she coaxed.

"Don' wanna five dollars," he whimpered.

"Here's ten dollars then."

"Don' wanna ten dollars."

"Well, what do you want?" asked the nurse crossly.

"I want my bat."

A doctor in New York for a medical convention was conversing with a gorgeous blond in the lobby of the Plaza when his wife suddenly emerged from the elevator. Eying the departing figure, the wife snapped, "How do you happen to know her?"

"Oh, just professionally," the doctor replied.

The wife raised a sarcastic eyebrow. "Yours, or hers?" she asked.

"You're going to like daddy."

The little boy was teaching the little girl next door a new game, "Pregnant."

"It's easy," he explained. "We go into the bathroom. I'll shave and you throw up."

Frustration: Finding out for the first time, you can't do it the second time. Panic: Finding out for the second time, you can't do it the first time.

"You keep out of it, this is just between your mother and me!"

GEORGE WHITE

The inroads of television have doubled unemployment among film actors. For example, the movie producer who came home early one night and found his wife in the arms of a one-time B-movie hero, Rock Bottomly.

"Hey!" cried the upset producer. "What are you doing?"

Rock's manly brow knotted in concern. "To tell you the truth," he said earnestly, "not much of anything these days."

The wife was understandably furious when she came home unexpectedly and found her husband in bed with a lady midget.

"You promised me two weeks ago that you would never cheat on me again," she stormed.

Her husband shrugged nonchalantly. "Take it easy, dear," he said airily. "Can't you see I'm tapering off?!"

"I don't think you really wanted your football sweater back at all."

The built blonde greeted her date in a strapless dress with no visible means of support. "Wow-ee," whistled her ecstatic escort, "I don't see what keeps that dress up."

"You may, if you're lucky," she smiled.

Two pro golfers were making money during their vacation by hanging around the local courses and betting with unsuspecting vacationers. An elegant-looking duffer drove up alone and to the two pros he looked like an easy mark. The pros flipped a coin and the winner approached the duffer. "I'm alone," said the pro, "would you like some company?"

The duffer agreed and as they approached the first tee, the pro suggested they make the game interesting and play for 'something.' "Okay," said the duffer, "but you pros don't fool me a bit. We'll play for a hundred dollars a hole and you'll give me a two goose handicap."

"Two goose handicap?" enquired the pro, "I know what a two stroke handicap is, but what is a two goose handicap?" The duffer explained that he needed no extra strokes, but according to the rules of the two goose handicap, he, the duffer, was allowed to stand behind the pro at every stroke but had only two chances to utilize his handicap.

On the first tee, one of the "handicap" strokes was used resulting in a slice into the woods.

After the game, it was a harried-looking pro who flopped into a club house chair beside his friend.

"Well, how much did you take the sucker for?" asked the friend.

"He took me for eighteen hundred dollars," was the unhappy reply; the pro proceeded to explain the handicap to his friend.

"Yes, but he had only two chances; he used one," his buddy replied. "How did he possibly get that much from you?"

"Have you ever played seventeen holes waiting for that second goose?"

Ya' know what they call a Jewish boy that joins a Monastry? A Schmunk.

Since the pretty young thing was warned by her mother not to go to strange young men's apartments, she only goes with those who act familiar.

It was a swinging party — lots of chicks, booze and dim lights. Orville Fenderlob was aware of a particularly nifty dish sitting alone in a corner. He went over, clapsed her in his arms and began kissing her passionately.

"Stop you fool!" she shrieked angrily, fighting herself loose from his arms.

"Pardon me," Orville bluffed smoothly, "I thought you were my sister."

"You idiot," she shot back, "I **am.**"

A colonel and major were dining in a Washington cafe and noticed a lovely morsel sitting with a PFC nearby. The colonel's fascination prompted him to send this note to the private:

"I believe I studied with you at Yale and the Major thinks he studied with you at Princeton. Please come over and straighten us out."

The private replied by note:

"I didn't study at Yale or Princeton, but I DID study at the National School of Taxidermy and I'm stuffing and mounting this pigeon myself!"

"Didn't you get my note?"

MIXED EMOTIONS: Watching your mother-in-law drive over a cliff in your brand new Thunderbird.

Guy: "What has red eyes, hundreds of legs, and a yellow back with black stripes?"

Gal: "I give up. What is it?"

Guy: 'I don't know, either, but I watched it crawl up your leg until it disappeared beneath your dress!"

"Frankly, we didn't expect neighbors to come calling so soon."

The woman had had a physical checkup on her 38th birthday, and the doctor now looked up from her X-Rays to say, "Mrs. Hammersmith, these X-Rays reveal a rather serious condition. I'm afraid you'll have to refrain from relationships with your husband for the next three months."

"That's just fine, Doctor," she replied, "Now I'll have more time for my boy friends."

A young virgin, suffering from acute nervousness due to repressed desires, paid a visit to a highly recommended psychiatrist. The doctor took one look at the voluptuous maiden and lost all his professional objectivity. "Take off your clothes," he ordered, in a voice that trembled slightly. "Now lie down on this couch, close your eyes and, very slowly, spell the word 'bedroom'. She began: "B...E...D...R...Oh! ...Ohh...Mmmmmm."
From that point on she was cured.

"Evelyn! Do you know where girls who act like that usually end up? In the hospital with pneumonia, that's where."

Then there was the sadist who found out his girl looked lousy in stripes — so he stopped whipping her.

TAXIDERMIST: A man who mounts animals.

"I'm looking for a girl who can do everything and also type."

A man walked into a doctor's office with the worst case of trembling hands the doctor had ever seen. "Tell me," the doctor said, "how long have you been shaking like this?"

"For years, Doc," the patient answered, "but it's much worse lately."

"Perhaps you drink too much," the doctor mused.

"I don't know," the patient said. "What's too much?"

"Oh, say a quart a day," the doctor replied.

"A quart a day!" the man exclaimed. "Good gosh, Doc, I spill that much!"

The Madison Avenue exec was dallying with both his secretary and the French maid, and on this particular evening he called home to make his excuses for a night out with the secretary. Fifi, the French maid, answered the phone and the executive said in a very business-like manner, "Tell Madam she'd better go to bed and I'll be along as soon as I can." **"Oui, Monsieur,"** purred Fifi, "and who shall I say is calling?"

Maryanne phoned her boyfriend and anxiously told him the news. "I've had morning sickness for several days. What should I do?" she wailed. An answer came quickly. "Work nights."

It was New Year's Eve and the house was brightly decorated with holiday trappings. The only sound that broke the quiet was the click of Grandma's knitting needles. The children; Jane, eight and Mary, five, were seated in front of a cheerily burning fire, leafing through a picture book. Tiring of this, they went over to Grandma's rocker. Jane climbed up on the arm of the chair and Mary snuggled into Grandma's cozy lap.

"Tell us a story," begged Mary.

"Oh," said the old lady, laying aside her knitting and wrapping her arms around the children. "What should I tell you about?"

"Tell us our favorite story," whispered little Jane eagerly. "About the time you were a whore in Chicago."

"A second honeymoon, **what** are you a sadist?"

INCOMPATABILITY: Two people who can't stomach each other.

Three girls and a man were brought before the presiding judge. The girls had been arrested for soliciting and the man was arrested for peddling without a license.

"What do you do for a living?" the judge asked, pointing to the first girl. "Your honor, I'm a model," she answered.

"Thirty days," was the sentence. Then he turned to the second. "What do you do for a living?" he asked.

"Your honor, I'm a T.V. actress."

"Thirty days." Then he turned to the third girl. "What do you do for a living?" he demanded.

"To tell you the truth," she answered, "I'm a prostitute."

"For telling the truth," he said, "I'm going to suspend sentence." Then he turned to the little peddler. "And you," he said, "what do you do for a living?"

"To tell you the truth," the peddler said, twisting his hat in his hands, "I'm a prostitute also."

Did you hear about the mixed-up Indian that couldn't tell heads from tails? Man!...you should see his crazy scalp collection.

Definition of a problem drinker: one who never buys.

BETTER LATE THAN NEVER... especially if you're a single girl!

Said the attractive, cigar-smoking housewife to her girl-friend: "I got started one night when George came home and found one burning in the ashtray."

"Oh, now I see why you Earthmen need two hands."

The elderly gentleman was nearing eighty but refused to accept his loss of sexual desire and stamina. He consulted with his doctor.

The doctor was amused and asked "Why should you be so concerned? It's expected at your age."

"But," pursued the oldster, "a friend of mine who is eighty-five says he makes love to his wife every night."

The doctor smiled. "Well, can't you say the same thing?"

They were going to a costume party. He was dressed as a caveman and she was decked out as a cow. A few miles from their destination, the car broke down and they were forced to walk across a field. They had gotten half way across when the wife shouted, "Henry, that bull looks like he's charging right for me. What'll I do?"

Henry replied, "Brace yourself!"

"Stop it or I'll scream!"

Have you heard about the dame at the plane factory who thought a tail assembly was the company picnic?

Oh, give me a home where the book-
makers roam,
Where the beer and the whiskey
flows free.
Where seldom is heard, a nice clean
word,
And the Callgirls keep calling for me.

"Have you been waiting long, dear?"

Expectant Father: "This is my first
baby."
Old Hand: "This is our seventh."
Expectant Father: "Well, gee, maybe
you can answer a question for me.
How soon after my wife has the baby
can she and I, uh—, you know what
I mean."
Old Hand: "That depends on
whether she is in a ward or a private room."

The 6:05 evening commuters' train was very late in leaving the station for its suburban destination. Jack and Frank were taking advantage of the wait in the station bar. They had, in fact, been drinking long enough to have reached the semi maudlin stage of confessing their individual sex lives.

"Do you know, pal," said Frank, "I never had any relations with my wife at all before we were married. Did you?"

Jack reflected for a moment and under the circumstances, with admirable sobriety, finally answered. "Gee, I dunno. What was her maiden name?"

"What makes you think there's someone else?"

Definition of a great lover: A guy who can breathe through his ears.

"The bridal suite...and hurry."

A class of six year olds were being taught words by the teacher. The word she used was 'frugal' and she explained that it meant 'to save' or 'saving.' Then to impress it on their memories she asked them to write a short story using the word. Little Jerry Finster wrote thusly:
"Once upon a time there was a beautiful young princess who was walking in the woods one day and happened to meet a young handsome prince. 'Oh, sir,' cried the princess, 'will you please frugal me? Please frugal me?' So the prince frugalled her and they lived happily ever after."

It happened in a medical clinic in the Mountain district of Arkansas. A mother entered with a rather large three year old and proceeded to nurse him, to the consternation of the staff.

"My dear woman," sputtered the doctor in charge, "that boy is too big to be nursed. You should have weaned him long ago." "I know," replied the mother, sadly. "But every time I try, he throws rocks at me."

"Your wife is a quite gifted conversationalist, Huntley."

Two jets passed two crows. Said one crow, "They were really going, weren't they?"

Said the other crow, "You would be going too if you had two A holes and they were both on fire."

HERMIT: A guy who goes off by himself.

"And if you want to remain head of the drafting department, Farnsworth, you'd better think twice before you fire anyone in the middle of the day like this, without first consulting me."

The son had been studying a course in Biology, bringing home dozens of books on matters pertaining to sex. His mother, finding the books and glancing through them became appalled that her little son, her own flesh and blood could become so involved with this dirty literature.

The husband arrived home and she could hardly restrain herself from becoming hysterical. She showed him the books and commanded him to go to the child's room and reprimand him.

The father, a rather typical American dad, genuinely frightened of his children, walked into the boy's room and found him in bed with the maid.

Standing in the doorway, he surveyed the scene, and off-handedly remarked: "Son, when you finish with your homework, I want a few words with you."

The farmer had borrowed a bull from a neighbor to service his two cows. He put the beast in the pasture and instructed his son to keep an eye on them. "As soon as the bull has finished let me know," he said. When the farmer got back to the house, he found the Reverend there on a social call. While they were sipping tea in the front room, the boy burst into the room. "Dad, Dad!" he exclaimed, "the bull just — — the brown cow!"

Greatly embarrassed, the farmer took his son outside. "Is that any way to talk in front of the Reverend?" he demanded to know. "Why couldn't you have said the bull **surprised** the brown cow. I would've understood. Now go back down to the pasture and come tell me when the bull is finished."

A few minutes later the boy again burst into the room.

"Dad, Dad—" he exclaimed.

"I know, I know," the father broke in hastily, "the bull has **surprised** the white cow."

"He sure has," exclaimed the excited boy, "he ————— the brown cow again!"

A shapely young girl from Lynn,
    Mass.
Has a really magnificent ass;
Not rounded and pink,
As you probably think—
It's gray, has long ears and eats
    grass.

Three newly-wed couples checked into a Niagara Falls hotel at the same time and the husbands happened to meet the next afternoon in the hotel bar. The conversation inevitably got around to the previous night's amorous activities. The first husband stated that he had made love to his wife five times between dusk and dawn. The second husband commented that he had lost count and got no sleep at all. When the third husband remained silent, the other two finally asked: "How many times did you go last night?"

"Just once," was the reply. "She wasn't used to it."

"This was so sudden!"

The father, who had been around, was having a heart-to-heart talk with his son before the boy's marriage. "Son," he said, "I have but two bits of advice to give you before you get married. First, insist right from the start on spending one night each week with the boys."

"And what," asked the son, "is the second bit of advice?"

His father smiled, and answered, "Don't waste it on the boys!"

"The pencils are 10c, Sir. And for a nominal service charge of $5.00 you are entitled to come up to my room and use my pencil sharpener."

"Your husband appears to be an awfully intelligent chap. Gives one the feeling that he knows everything."

"Don't worry. He doesn't suspect a thing!"

1st Cat: I'm going to have kittens and they'll be Angoras.

2nd Cat: I'm going to have kittens too, only I don't know what they'll be.

1st Cat: What do you mean, you don't know what they'll be?

2nd Cat: I had my head in a salmon can at the time!

"You're a good influence on me, Miss Tucker—you make me think big."

"Sam," his dying partner wheezed, "I have a confession to make. I robbed our firm of $100,000. I sold the secret formula to our competitors. I took the letter from your desk that your wife needed to get her divorce. And Sam, I . . ."

"That's all right, old man. It was me that poisoned you!"

The stress and strain of business was beginning to tell on Paul. He had learned to unwind each evening by relaxing with a martini in his den while reading Jackie Kannon's "Poems for the John." Unfortunately, his pretty, but not too bright, wife was not sensitive to Paul's tensions. This evening, just as he was getting comfortable, she breezed into his retreat wearing her toreador pants and climbed onto his lap. She cuddled, murmured and fondled, until he finally exploded:

"Good heavens, Cynthia, get off! I get enough of this at the office."

Bringing your wife to a convention is like taking the game warden hunting.

The inmates of a mental institution were listening raptly to some modern jazz records when one patient could contain himself no longer. Leaping to his feet he started to bang his head against the wall in tune to the music. Beating their hands together, the other inmates shouted, "Sane, man, sane!"

The newly-arrived ambassador to a Far Eastern country called on the Emperor to present his credentials. Although he was disturbed by the presence of so many comely, half-nude maidens in the palace, he was determined not to show it. Trying to restrict the conversation to affairs of state, he asked, "Your Highness, when was the last time you had an election?"

"Ah," said the Emperor, with a smile and a sly wink, "just befo' blekfast."

Our dictionary defines a Texan as a wet-back that didn't make it to Oklahoma.

"How do you catch rabbits?"
"I dunno. How?"
"Hide behind a tree and make noises like a carrot."

Husband: "I was an idiot when I married you."
Wife: "That's right, but I was too infatuated to notice!"

Two Brooklyn secretaries saved and pooled all their money to fly to Paris. Finally, after years, they made it. Everything was going along well until the last day of their visit when Mabel came into the room clutching the guidebook and looking very despondent.

"What's the matter, Mabel?" asked her friend.

"Do you happen to realize that we've been here two weeks and I haven't been to the Louvre," answered Mabel.

"It's probably something in the water," replied her friend.

"I read about them somewhere...but I don't remember what they were used for!"

HOME COOKING: Where many a man thinks his wife is.

Joe and Mervin, both expectant fathers, were pacing the waiting room floor.

"What rotten luck," grumbled Joe. "This was supposed to be my vacation."

"You think you've got troubles," retorted Mervin. "This is my **honeymoon!**"

"Think of me as someone to love, someone to confide in; forget that I'm your wife."

The Dean of Women at a prominent college was introducing a visiting dignitary to the student body. In tones of admiration, bordering on awe, she said, "I couldn't begin to list the accomplishments of our honored guest, but as an indication you'll be interested to know that he has a nine-inch **Who's Who.**"

WAVE officers have a difficult time enforcing orders about wearing only regulation 'Navy issue' items. A male supply officer on this particular post had to enforce these rules and one day he had to consult the WAVE officer in order to ensure that the regulations were carried out. He thought he would save time by going to visit the officer in WAVE headquarters. Not certain of the way into the building he started down a hallway and came to an open door... and stood rooted to the spot. It was a washroom and busy at the wash basin was a nude WAVE. Before the man could collect his wits, the girl turned around and saw him. The man waited, speechless, for the shriek of alarm.

"You'll notice, sir," said the girl sweetly, "strictly WAVE items."

"I had a fine time, Mr. Morton—Once I got loaded!"

DIVORCE: Going through a change of wife.

A man is getting old when he can't take "Yes" for an answer.

"Well, now —this looks like a good spot."

An elderly bull's days of love-making were, alas, behind him, but the tender-hearted farmer let him remain in the pasture with the cows he could no longer service. But the farmer, having a head for business, bought a young bull and turned him loose in the pasture. Noting his young rival, the old timer began to snort and paw the turf.

"Stop working yourself up," the farmer told him. "You're too old for that kind of stuff."

"Maybe I am," answered the bull, "but at least I can show him I'm not a cow, can't I?"

January 1, 1962

Dear Wife:

During the past year I have attempted to seduce you 365 times. I succeeded 26 times. This averages once every two weeks.

The following list gives the reasons for my failure:

We will wake the children	7
It's too hot	15
It's too cold	5
Too tired	99
It's too early	16
It's too late	23
Pretending sleep	60
Window open, neighbors will hear	9
Backache	16
Headache	2
Giggles	10
I'm too full	4
Not in the mood	24
Baby crying	20
Mud pack	19
Company in the guest room	3
You're too drunk	7
TOTAL	**339**

Do you think we could improve our record this coming year?

Hopefully,
Your loving husband

Then there was the chap who went to a quiet farmhouse to get a rest and fell into a half filled cesspool on his first night walk over the grounds. "Help!" he shouted, "Fire! Fire!"

In a short time the firemen, policemen and all the other guests arrived and dragged him besmirched and forlorn from the smelly pit.

"What's the idea of yelling Fire," demanded the Chief. "There's no fire here."

"What you want me to holler?" answered the irate guest. "Crap?"

"Wouldn't it be wonderful if we could turn this into a mail order business?"

Lady Burnside sat on her backside,
Dusting her frontside with peroxide.
For she knew on the whole,
Gentlemen prefer blondes.

"You're probably asking yourself what all this has to do with your dog's distemper—"

It was in a bar in midtown Manhattan and the Frenchman and the American were talking about love over some dry Martinis.

"Deed you know, sir," the Frenchman said, "that een my country thair are 79 different ways how to make the REAL, passionate luff."

"Do tell?" said the American. "Well, that's amazing. In my country there's only one."

"Just one?" the Frenchman said, saucer-eyed. "And what eez that?"

"Well, there's a man and there's a woman, and —"

"Sacre bleu!" said the Frenchman. "Numbair 80!"

A gentleman whose wife delivered a boy seven months after marriage, asked his physician the reason for this.

"Don't worry about it," said the Doctor, "this often happens in the case of the first child, but never afterwards."

"Eat the right food, keep your weight down, and get yourself a good lawyer."

Fifteen year old Sammy came running out of a burlesque show where he had just seen a stripper in action. "Why are you in such a hurry?" asked the Manager.

The young man skidded to a stop and replied excitedly—"My mother told me that if I ever looked at anything bad I would turn to stone—and I've started!"

A Marine regiment was sent back for rest after a tough tour of duty at the front. At the base they discovered a contingent of WACs billeted and awaiting assignments to various posts. The Marine colonel addressed himself to the WAC commander, warning her that his men had been in the front lines a long time and might not be too careful about their attitudes toward the WACs.

"If you don't want any trouble," he told the WAC commander grimly, "you better keep 'em locked up."

"Trouble?" she echoed. "There'll be no trouble. My girls have it up here." And she tapped her forehead significantly.

"I don't care where they have it," barked the Colonel, "my boys will find it unless they're locked up."

"Did you hear the one about the sultan who left a call for eight in the morning?"

"Does your girl smoke?"
"Not quite!"

Once upon a girl there was a time...

How does a deserving girl get herself a mink?
The same way minks do.

The time had come. He had shown her his etchings and everything else of interest in the apartment; now the moment of truth had arrived.

"Tell me," he said smoothly, fingering a lock of her hair, "do you object to making love?"

She turned her lovely eyes up to his.

"That's something I've never done," she said.

"Never made love?" he cried, appalled at the waste of his careful preparations.

"No, silly," she cooed. "Never objected!"

"For gosh sakes! Why don't you let a pal know when you're coming home. I'd have been glad to drive out to the airport and and pick you up."

African Roulette: You get in bed with six beautiful african girls, one of them is a cannibal.

She snuggled in his arms, raised her head and kissed his eyelids, nibbled his ear, bit him on the shoulder. Looking up at him, she said: "You know, I've never done anything like this before?"

"Well!" he replied, "You certainly inherited a load of talent."

"What's your name, stupid?"

BUYING FIRST-CLASS MERCHANDISE IS SIMILAR TO BUYING GRAIN. If you desire fresh, clean, first quality grain you always have to pay a reasonable and fair price. However, if you can be content with grain that has already been through the horse . . . WELL, THE PRICE OF THAT IS A BIT CHEAPER.

A hotel served two private luncheons; one to a group of clergymen, the other to a meeting of wholesale liquor dealers. The dealers ordered a special dessert; watermelon soaked with brandy, rum and benedictine. The manager of the hotel discovered to his horror that there had been a mix-up and the spiked melon had been served to the ministers.

"What did they say?" he asked the headwaiter. "Were there any complaints?"

"They didn't say a word," the man reported. "They were too busy putting the seeds in their pockets!"

Then there was the pregnant nurse whose theme song was "Witch Doctor"?

"His family wasn't too pleased to hear of our engagement—especially his wife."

For five years of married life the Office Casanova had been unable to produce a child. Naturally, since he was so constantly boasting of his virility, he was subject to much ribbing about his impotence.

One day, after receiving so much teasing from his co-office workers, he proudly announced that his wife had been to the doctor and that the doctor had definitely confirmed that fact that his wife was pregnant.

"So what?" said one of the fellows. "None of us ever doubted your wife's ability . . ."

"I need a camel that can go without water for at least three weeks," the American said to an Algerian camel merchant. "Is it possible?"

"All things are possible," replied the merchant. He proceeded to take a camel out of his barn and lead him to a tank of water. After the camel had drunk its fill and was about to lift its head out of the tank, the merchant picked up two nearby bricks, one in each hand, ran behind the camel and whacked him in the testicles.

The camel let out a gigantic "Whoosh!" and sucked up what seemed like 20 more gallons of water.

The American stared incredulously at the camel merchant. "My God, man!" he exclaimed, "doesn't that hurt?!"

The merchant shrugged. "Only if you get your thumbs in between the bricks."

One he-male to another: "I love to hear girlish laughter, but not from my partner."

Taking your wife to a convention is like bringing a sandwich to a banquet.

1st Divorcee: "How did you get **your** divorce?"

2nd Ditto: "It wasn't hard."

Farmer Jones was a cold, dispassionate man. It was fully six months after the wedding that the marriage was consummated, and it was an odd, spur of the moment act.

He had been plowing the south forty when he suddenly called out to his bride in a shrieking voice and ran madly across the field. Swooping her up in his arms, he carried her into the house and made violent love.

The identical act was repeated approximately a year later.

Another six months went by and one afternoon Mrs. Jones heard the shrieking call. She ran out of the house with arms outstretched expectantly.

"Sex maniac!" he flung at her. "The barn's on fire!"

"Actually I didn't go into this business intentionally. It started out as just a hobby."

A definition of slipcover: A maternity dress.

Screen Writer: But boss, you can't make a movie out of that book. It's about Lesbians!

Movie Producer: So who cares? We'll re-write the script and make them Americans!

"Somehow it's just not the same. Let's go out and get in the back seat of the car."

A lady from Chicago was visiting New York City. Her hostess was determined to make the Midwesterner feel cheap and unimportant.

"My dear," said the New York matron snobbishly, "here in the East, we think breeding is everything."

The lady from the Midwest answered, "Oh, I don't know. Out where I come from we think it's fun, too, but we try to have a few outside interests as well."

For some time the teen-age girl had been troubled with coughing spells so she was taken by her mother to see a doctor. He explained that in order to make a proper diagnosis he would have to examine the girl's chest.

Placing his stethoscope above her heart, he said, "Big breaths."

"Yeth," she replied proudly, "and I'm only thixteen!"

"I don't know, Sir. Nobody has ever charged it to a credit card before."

After the appropriate amount of wining and dining, the surprised young bachelor couldn't even collect a goodnight kiss. Wide-eyed, she coyly explained, "I never kiss on the first date." "Well honey," he deep-breathed, "What about on the last?"

Butch Fagan was a real rugged, loud mouthed individual. He was hospitalized for the first time in his life and was the lone occupant of a semi-private room. The very first day, he felt an urge for the latrine, and rather loudly called:

"Hey, nurse, I have to take a _____."

The nurse was shocked by his use of the uncouth word and sternly said,

"Don't use that expression. Whenever this situation arises, I want you to say, 'number two'."

The man said he would and he did. The next day, a new patient was assigned to the room and after a while informed Butch that he needed the facilities of the bathroom. Whereupon Butch yelled for the nurse, and then told her:

"Hey, this guy has to take a _____, give him a number."

"For some reason I don't feel non-objective today, Miss Kopacks."

"Mind if I skip you? I promised my wife I'd be home early!"

A young boy of seven went to a movie and saw a picture co-starring Marilyn Monroe and Marlon Brando. In one passionate scene, Marlon tore off Marilyn's blouse and said: "I want what I want when I want it!" This idea really caught on with the small boy and he ran right home to try it out on the little girl next door. The first thing he did when he arrived at her house was to call her out into the yard, rip off her blouse and say, "I want what I want when I want it!" The surprised six-year-old girl looked at him squarely and retorted, "You'll get what I got when I get it!"

The switchboard operator in a swank New York hotel received a call at 2 A.M. from a somewhat inebriated man who wanted to know what time the hotel bar opened.

"At 9 A.M., sir," she replied.

At 3:15 A.M. the phone rang again, and the drunk repeated his question, his speech considerably thicker than before.

"Not until 9 A.M., sir," she said a second time, a trace of impatience in her voice.

At 5:30 A.M. she received another call from the same guy, now completely stoned.

"I told you, sir," she snapped, "you'll have to wait until 9 A.M. to get into the bar."

"Get in, Hell," croaked the drunk, "I want to get **out!**"

The trouble is that we take all our daytime problems to bed with us. There's only one solution, get our wives to sleep out.

Sex is the most fun you can have without laughing.

Definition of a prophylactic: A thinking man's filter.

FOR EVERY MAN THERE'S A WOMAN . . . and if his wife ever knew about it, she'd kill him!

Cockeyed Sally was shapely but shy, and visited a doctor for the first time. He ushered her into his private office, and said:

"And now, my dear, please get completely undressed."

Sally blushed and replied, "OK, doctor, but you first!"

"He's on his vacation."

A newly wedded husband stopped at his druggist for a refill on an order of sleeping pills. "I don't know what I'd ever do without them. I'd never get any rest."

"Don't take too many," cautioned the pharmacist.

"Me?" said the husband in surprise. "Never use them. I give them to my wife!"

"Doctor," she asked anxiously, "am I finally cured?"

"Yes, Miss Jones," replied the analyst. "I feel that we have your kleptomania under control and you can go out in to the world like anyone else."

"Oh, Doctor, I'm so grateful," said the woman. "I don't know how I can ever repay you for all you have done for me."

"My fee is ample payment," said the analyst. "However, if you should happen to have a relapse, you might pick up a small transistor radio for my son."

"Oh, Harold, let's not spoil the sweet, wonderful magic of this day, by ending it on a vulgar note."

SCREWBALL . . . A dance held in a bordello.

Father to Buxom College Daughter: Who was that fellow I saw making love to you last night?

Buxom College Daughter: What time was it?

"You said I could have the maid for a party."

A young couple were at the village town hall to apply for a marriage license.

"Name?" asked the clerk.

"Isiah Smith."

"Your name?" he asked the girl.

"Mary Lou Smith."

"Oh," the clerk paused. "Any connection?"

The boy and girl looked at each other and blushed furiously. Finally Isiah stammered out: "Yes, but only twice."

Most nurses, generally speaking, are easy-going sort of people, able to withstand the numerous stresses of their profession. But if anything gets their dander up, it's working with a tyrannical, inconsiderate doctor. Four nurses, assigned to such a doctor's patients, decided at long last to retaliate and teach their doctor boss a lesson. They each planned a separate surprise for him, and when all the four plots were put into operation, they met to discuss their respective bits of skulduggery.

"I stuffed cotton in the bottom of his stethoscope," the first said proudly. "Is he going to get a surprise when he examines his patients tomorrow morning!"

"He sure will," the second agreed. "I let the mercury out of all his thermometers, and painted them to read 108."

The third giggled: "I did even better than that. I went through his desk and found his private box of contraceptives. I took a pin and punched holes in every one of them."

The fourth nurse fainted.

Side by side they relaxed in bed, contentedly dragging on their cigarettes. Finally one of them broke the silence.

"You know," he said, "this wife-swapping wasn't such a bad idea. I only hope our wives are hitting it off this well!"

A young New York housewife was shocked by some of the language used by her little daughter. When asked about it, the daughter said she had learned it from a small girl she played with in the Park.

The next day the mother sought out the little girl as she played in the Park.

"Are you the little girl who uses bad words?"

"Who told you?"

"A little bird," answered the mother.

"Well, I like that!" exclaimed the small girl. "And I've been feeding the little bastards, too!"

"Now, if you'll just lie down here, I'd like to give you one more test on what you're best suited for."

CONTINENTAL BREAKFAST: A roll in bed with some honey.

An insanely jealous woman compelled her husband to undergo a rigid inspection after every "night out with the boys." If she discovered a single hair on his clothes, there would be a terrible row. One night, having found nothing, not even a single hair, she burst into tears and cried: "Even bald-headed women, now!"

"...and I said to myself, 'So the groom didn't show up—that's not going to ruin my day'."

As she nervously held him off, the young chick whispered:
"You'll have to be patient; you must give me time."
He: "How much, a day? A week? A month?"
She: "Just wait 'til the moon gets behind that cloud!"

Her eyes, filled with tears,
Susan confessed her tearful tidings
to her mother.
"Mom" she said, "I'm pregnant."
"Ye Gods!" screamed her mother.
"Who is the father?"
She lifted her weeping face. "How
should I know?" she wailed. "You
never would let me go steady."

"Miss Tucker, I've been noticing you."

Wee Willie was walking with Shirley,
his new girlfriend, carrying her books
home from grammar school. Both
were eight years old.
"Shirley," said Wee Willie with wor-
shipping gaze, "you are the first girl
I have ever loved."
"Dammit," said Shirley, "I've drawn
another beginner!"

A local bank failed and there was a wildly cursing, milling mob of frantic depositors pounding on the doors. In the center of this half-crazed, shouting crowd was one fellow running his mouth louder than the rest. "They should string up the president of this bank to a lamp post...also the board of trustees! To take the poor depositors' hard earned cash ...the poor depositors now left without homes or bread...We should send the bank officials to Siberia to the salt mines...the dirty crooks!" Finally a policeman walked over to him and asked, "Look, mister, have you got any money in this bank, may I ask...?"

"Listen, officer," came the guy's answer, "if I had any money in this bank, would I be taking it so lightly?"

The car had just come to a sudden stop against a telephone pole, and the driver sat cursing the safety belt that still bound him to the seat. The policeman investigating the accident was understandably confused.

"Holy smoke, Mac," he exclaimed, "if you hadn't been wearing that safety belt you'd have followed that young lady right through the windshield. So why are you blamin' your safety belt for what happened?"

"Are you kiddin'?" groaned the driver. "Look what she's got in her hand!"

The Texan was beginning to wear on his listeners with his bragging when one spoke up and said: "Yep, those Texans are big people, all right. I knew one so big that when he died they couldn't find a coffin big enough to bury him in so they gave him an enema and buried him in a shoe box."

"He was the hardest man to please I've ever waited on."

There was a knock on the door. Mrs. Miffin opened it.

"Are you the Widow Miffin?" a small boy asked.

"I'm Mrs. Miffin," she replied, "but I'm not a widow."

"Oh, no?" replied the little boy. "Wait 'til you see what they're carrying upstairs!"

An avid health addict was telling a friend why he was so wide awake in the early morning. "Yes, I've learned that the best way to start a day is to exercise ten minutes, take a deep breath of fresh air, and finish with a cold shower. Then I feel rosy all over."

Suddenly the friend looked interested. "Tell me more about this Rosy."

"You're just supposed to **kiss** the bride, Johnson."

Here's to the girl that's sweet,
Here's to the girl that's true,
Here's to the girl in all our hearts...
In other words, it's about 2 A.M., fellows, what do you say we all go down to Madame LaSexe's for the remainder of the night?

Henrietta was a pretty young lady in the blush of her eighteenth year. She had been away at college for about three months, then one day she unexpectedly came home. Her mother greeted her at the door, and asked the reason for this sudden return.

"I might as well tell you now, Mother," Henrietta said. "I'm going to have a baby."

Her mother seemed quite calm. "Now, dear, you must promise not to say anything about this to your father. You know how nervous he is, and this might cause him to have a breakdown."

"All right, Mother," Henrietta agreed.

"And," her mother continued, "you must not breathe a word of this to your brother. He has a big mouth and if he knows he'll tell the whole neighborhood."

"I promise," Henrietta promised. "But what about you, Mother, haven't you anything to say?"

Her mother was silent for a moment. Then she said, "No. I'm not going to make a scene. I'm just going to walk into the bedroom and quietly commit suicide."

A delinquent customer received the following letter from a creditor:

"Dear Sir: After checking our records we have concluded that we have done more for you than your mother ever did—we've carried you for fifteen months!"

The nurse was understandably skeptical when the newly-arrived patient explained that his broken leg was the result of something that happened twenty years before.

"But it's true," insisted the patient. "I went to work for a farmer twenty years ago, and the first night after I went to bed, the farmer's beautiful daughter came into my room fully dressed and asked if I wanted anything. I said, 'No.'

"The second night she came again, and this time she was clad in a negligee. Again she asked if I wanted anything, and again I told her 'No.'

"The third night when she came in she was entirely nude. 'Are you sure you don't want anything?' she inquired warmly. 'Positive,' I said. 'I've had a good supper, the bed is comfortable and I feel fine.'

"By that time I couldn't help wondering what she thought I could possibly want. Then, yesterday, as I was shingling the roof, it came to me like a flash!"

The peace was shattered abruptly by the window of a local lodge being equally shattered. A policeman who arrived promptly on the scene demanded to know what was going on.

"Oh," said the man who greeted him, a trifle sheepishly. "We're just holding an Elk's ball."

"Then for the love of Heaven let him go," urged the policeman, "before he kicks the whole place down!"

Wife with hands cupped: "Guess what I've got in here and you can have a little piece tonight."
Husband after thinking real hard: "An elephant."
Wife: "That's close enough."

"I was sitting up with a lovesick friend!"

Did you hear about the poor guy who scrimped and saved for years to buy his mother a house. She was only open a week when they arrested her for running it.

Reassuring words to tell your date: "There's really nothing to worry about—I kid you not."

A group of one hundred freshmen from an upstate college each contributed $2 to the kitty. When the money was collected, they drew lots to see which one would have the pleasure of visiting the town's famous call girl who charged $200 a visit.

That night the winner, a pimply faced youth named Homer, went to her boudoir and handed her the money.

"That's a huge sum of money for a college boy to have," she told him.

He explained the entire situation to her, telling her how all the boys had drawn lots to see who would have the honor of partaking in her favors.

She was touched by the story. "I'm going to do something that I've never done before," she told him. "I'm going to give you back your money."

Then she gave him back his $2.

The farmer was priming his prize Brahma bull for the big county fair that was being held in two days. But when he looked the bull over in the pasture he nearly fainted because the animal's eyes were crossed. He ran to the house, made a frenzied call, and the local vet arrived inside of an hour. While the farmer gazed wide-eyed, the vet inserted a long glass tube into the bull's rump and blew with great gusto into the other end. In a moment the bull's eyes uncrossed.

"I'm leaving you this tube," said the vet, "just in case it happens again." Two mornings later the farmer looked at his highly-touted animal's eyes. They were crossed again.

Continued

He hollered for his stable-hand who came running with the vet's glass tube. Inserting the tube into the bull's backside as the vet had done, and instructing the hand to hold the bull's horns, the farmer took a deep breath and blew into the tube with all his might. Nothing happened.

Getting desperate now, the farmer said, "Clem, you do the blowin' and I'll hold the horns cause this durn animule might be particular who he's a-lookin at."

So he grabbed the horns and the stable-hand went to the rear where he extracted the tube, turned it around, put it back in, and started to blow into it.

"Now what in tarnation did you turn the tube around for Clem?" the farmer said.

"Gosh boss," said the stable-hand, "you don't think I'm gonna put my mouth on the same end you put yours!"

Three young rabbis were boasting to each other how progressive they were. "My synagogue is so modern, we have ash trays in all the pews." "That's nothing," said the second, "in my synagogue, we have a lunch counter that serves ham sandwiches after services." "You guys can't hold a candle to my congregation," said the third. "We're so reformed, we close for the Jewish holidays!"

The king had arranged a truly regal marriage for his daughter. She had married the crown prince of their rich and powerful neighboring country and this union held great promise to unite these two nations.

Although the king was delighted with the ceremony, he was bothered by the cold, correct formality with which the young couple treated each other. Troubled that the union may not be a success, he posted a spy outside of the bridal chamber to report on the wedding nights events.

The next morning the king's spy reported as follows: "I couldn't really tell how well they got along because of their odd behavior. As they entered the chamber the Princess said, "I offer you my honor" and the prince replied, "Madame, I honor your offer." And that is the way it went all night long— honor, offer, honor, offer."

Do you know what a super thief is? A super thief steals another man's wife a little piece at a time.

If all the girls in the world were blades of grass, what would all the boys be? Grasshoppers.

"You can relax . . . I'm a vegetarian."

It was at the eighth annual mouse convention and mice from near and far had gathered for the ball. A pretty little female mouse waltzed by the stag line and one of the males whistled a low, dirty whistle to himself. Turning to another male mouse he said, "Look at the legs on that mouse, aren't they beautiful?"

"Just fair," was the answer.

"You crazy," said the first mouse and then turning to another, asked his opinion.

"They're nice," said the third mouse, "but nothing to get excited about."

"Some mice have no appreciation," exclaimed the first mouse. "Now you," he said to a fourth mouse, "what do you think of them?"

"To tell the truth," was the reply, "I'm no authority on legs, I'm a titmouse myself."

"I'm sorry, but this isn't exactly what I thought you had in mind when you advertised for a girl for house work."

When Roxanne Trumbenik got to be 28 without any matrimonial prospects in sight, her mother goaded her into placing an ad in a lonely-hearts newspaper. The ad read:

"Beautiful, well-to-do young heiress seeks correspondence with devil-may-care gentleman who wants all that he can get out of life in a hurry."

They gave the ad a week's time to get results, and finally Mrs. Trumbenik asked anxiously, "Well? Any answers?"

"Just one," sighed Roxanne.

"Who wrote you?" demanded Mama.

"I don't think I should tell you," said the girl sadly.

"But this was my idea," shouted the mother, "and I insist that you tell me for-goodness sakes!"

"All right, you asked for it! It was from Papa!"

The soldier had just returned from two years service in Korea. After an exciting reunion with his wife they went immediately to a hotel. Later that night there was a loud knock on their door and a voice shouted "Let me in."

"Great Scott," exclaimed the soldier, as he bolted upright in bed, "I'll bet that's your husband!"

"Don't be silly," his wife sleepily reassured him, "he's in Korea!"

"After he gave me the pearls I realized he must have eaten a lot of oysters!"

Doctor: "Madame, I'd like to give you a thorough examination. Take off your clothes."
Patient: "But Dr. Kannon found me in perfect condition this Morning."
Doctor: "So he told me, so he told me."

"Don't be shy. As a doctor I have only a professional interest in your luscious, full, delightful body...."

On the pretext of securing some important contracts, the henpecked hubby had been spending the majority of his evenings away from home. When his wife discovered that he was really having secret rendezvous with a number of different lady friends, she confronted him with this accusation. Reluctantly, he admitted the truth. Then the worm started to turn. "So what?" he snarled, in a voice roughly approximating that of a B picture villain. "In fact, I have a date tonight. And you know who's gonna help me get dressed for my date? You are! And you know who's gonna shine my shoes? You are! And you know who's gonna tie my tie?"

"Yes," his wife said quietly, "the undertaker."

The famous athlete from an Ivy League College checked into the Mountain Hotel on his wedding night.

She was very shy when they were about to undress and asked him to wait in the bathroom until she got into her nightgown.

After a few minutes of panting behind the john door he called out "Ready, dear?" "Just a minute, honey," she replied. A few minutes later the same scene was repeated. Finally, he heard her call out "Ready, darling."

The bathroom door flew open, out flashed the athlete into the darkened bedroom, tripped over a chair and pole vaulted out the window.

"This is where they separate the men from the boys."

"Oh, brother! Now I suppose we'll have to listen to nine choruses of 'Cheating Heart'."

It was his first night in a strange town and he was understandably lonely. As he morosely sipped his Martini his glance was caught and held by a dazzling redhead at the other end of the bar who was quite apparently alone. Here, he thought, would be a charming companion for dinner.

He approached her, and exerting all the charm at his command, said, "Pardon me, but can I buy you a drink?"

She eyed him for a second, then in a voice that rocked every patron in the cocktail lounge, she cried, "WHA-AT? GO TO A HOTEL?!"

Continued

He was taken aback. "I didn't say that," he stammered, "I just asked you to have a drink with me."

"A MOTEL?!!!" she shrieked.

The bartender rushed over to him and bellowed, "What are you: some kind of a nut? We run a respectable place here so drink up and get out!"

Two minutes later he was on the street outside the cocktail lounge, a thoroughly confused young man. Determined to learn the reason for her extraordinary behavior he retraced his steps and appoached her again. This time she was the first to speak.

"I'm terribly sorry I spoke to you the way I did," she apologized, "but the truth is I'm a psychology major who has to prepare a thesis on the way men behave under embarrassing condi—"

"WHA-AT?!" cried the young man, as the still-crowded bar suddenly became silent. "FIFTY DOLLARS?!!"

The census taker viewed Mandy and the six tots of varying ages around her with a puzzled frown. He seemed particularly intrigued with a squirming infant in her arms. "I don't quite understand you," he admitted. "Did you say that your husband died six years ago?" "Yes, Sir," she replied emphatically. "He died but I didn't."

The timid young man and his pretty date were parked by the side of the road. Placing his hand on her thigh, he whispered, "I love you."

Quivering at his touch, she replied, "A little higher."

"I love you," came the higher-pitched reply.

"Answer my question truthfully now. Remember you are on your honor."

Man: "Doctor, I'm afraid you'll have to remove my wife's tonsils one of these days."

Doctor: "My good man, I removed them six years ago. Did you ever hear of a woman having two sets of tonsils!"

Man: "No, but you've heard of a man having two wives, haven't you?"

He: "Do you believe in free love?"
She: "Have I ever given you a bill?"

". . . and another old saying of ours is, 'Where there's a will, there's a way.'"

The fellow had wooed and won the love of his life, and decided it was time to take her home to meet his family. "This is my intended wife," he announced to his parents.

His father took him aside when the opportunity presented itself. "This girl doesn't look like much to me," he said.

"But, father," the boy said. "This girl is a baroness. Doesn't that impress you?"

"You mean," exclaimed the father, "that she can't have any children?"

A British gentleman who was riding in a cab in New York was challenged by the driver to solve a riddle: "This person I'm thinking of has the same father that I have and the same mother but it is not my sister and it's not my brother. Who is it?" The Britisher pondered seriously over the question and then gave up. "It's me," the cab driver told him.

"By Jove, that's a jolly smart one! I can't wait until I get back to London so I can try it on the chaps at my club!"

And so a month later, when he was sitting in his club back in London in a circle of his cigar-smoking cronies, he called them all to attention and recited the stickler to them.

"This individual I have in mind is not my brother and is not my sister, yet this person has the same parents as I have. Who is it?"

After several thoughtful minutes, all the members conceded defeat. "Who is it?" one of them inquired. "Come, Reggie, give us the solution." Reggie slapped his knee in triumph. "It's a taxicab driver in New York City!" he roared.

"Oh, Doctor," twittered the newly-married girl, "you must help me. Ever since you outfitted me with this diaphragm I urinate purple."

"Hm-m-m, what kind of jelly do you use?" asked the M.D. The bride looked wistfully and replied "Grape!"

Do you know what Ferdinand wanted for Xmas? A good tight Jersey.

An **optimist** is a husband who goes down to the marriage bureau to see if his license has expired.

"Charlie, you haven't been so much fun in twenty years!"

What is the difference between a peeping Tom and a pick-pocket? A pick-pocket snatches watches.

Did you hear about the preacher that ruined his organ on a hymm?

"Could I buy you a drink?" he asked, by way of striking up a conversation.

"No thank you," she said, "I don't drink."

"What about a little dinner with me in my room?"

"No, I don't believe that would be proper," she said.

Having had no success with the subtler approaches, the young man pressed directly to the point: "I am charmed by your refreshing beauty, mademoiselle, and will give you anything your heart desires if you will spend the night with me."

"Oh, no, no, monsieur, I could never do a thing like that."

"Tell me," the young man said, laughing, "don't you ever do anything the slightest bit improper?"

"Oui," said the French girl, "I tell lies."

"Oh, please don't get up. I can only stay a minute."

His young son had been acting a little strangely lately so he took him to a psychiatrist who proceeded to ask him a few questions.

"Tell me, son," he said paternally, "how many wheels does an auto have?"

The answer came promptly: "Four."

"Very good. Now what is it a cow has four of, that a woman has two?"

"Legs."

"And what does your father have that your mother likes most?"

"Money."

The psychiatrist turned to the father and said, "You don't have to worry about **him**...he's smart!"

The father nodded reluctantly. "He sure is! I missed the last two questions myself."

"I'm very sorry Paul," she said, "I can never learn to love you."
"Gee that's too bad," said Paul, "and after I'd saved twenty grand, too."
"Give me one more lesson."

"Now, Florence, what's this I hear about you sleeping on the job?"

Patient in Doctor's office: "I don't feel too well."
Doctor: "Strip to the waist and when I hit you on the back, cough."
The doctor hits him, he coughs. This continues for about 15 minutes. At last the doctor said to him: "How long have you had this cough?"

Three young ladies were taking the same course in logic at Wassar College. After one of the lectures, the professor posed a problem in situation reasoning.

"Let us imagine," said the prof, "that you were alone and adrift in a small boat on the high seas. Suddenly you see a passing liner with hundreds of sex starved sailors aboard. What would you do in this situation to avoid any problem?"

"I would turn my craft in the opposite direction," stated the blonde.

"I would pretend I was in a single-handed, transatlantic race," responded the brunette.

"Well," murmured the redhead, "I understand the situation, but fail to see the problem."

"Oh, excuse me doctor—I thought you were psychoanalyzing!"

It happened in Las Vegas at one of the posh gambling casinos.

One morning at about 3:00 A.M. a tall, beautiful blonde, wearing a full length sable coat walked up to the crap table. Plunking down $2,000.00, she picked up the dice and started to shake them vigorously, arm outstretched above her head. At this moment her coat opened and to the startled housemen revealed that under the sable she was completely nude.

Taking two steps back, she lifted her left leg, swung her arm underneath and tossed the dice on the table. She reached across the table, exposing her beautiful breasts, picked up the dice and hurled them against the backboard. "Four," she yelled, collected the money on the table, buttoned her coat and walked out of the casino. One of the dazed housemen looked at the other and asked "Was four her point?" With a vacant stare the other replied. "I don't know, I thought **you** were watching!"

The young girl had not been feeling well and went to her family doctor. "Young lady," said the doctor, "you're pregnant." "But that can't be. The only men I've been with are nudists and in our colony we practice sex only with our eyes." "Well, my dear," said the doctor, "someone in that colony is cockeyed."

"May I use your phone?"

"Police Station? I want to report a wild party at 3412 Elm Street."

Man at a bar complaining to another and sobbing hysterically, "My wife just left me and I can't control my emotions. I just can't control my emotions."

Second Man: "Why bother? Let yourself go, you'll feel better after a good laugh!"

"Martha! Junior's drawing on the walls again!"

A woodpecker came to Texas from another State and was up a tree pecking away. While doing this, lightning struck the tree splitting it down the middle. "It beats hell how hard your pecker can get when you're away from home," he said.

SPEAK SOFTLY AND CARRY A BIG STICK...and they'll think you're queer!

"Are you decent?"

Nobody expected the Jukes' shiftless son to amount to a hill of beans but he astounded the whole neighborhood one day, by getting the daughter of the richest man in town to marry him. The ceremony took place in the biggest church in town. Everything went smoothly and the young man slipped the ring on his girl's finger, saying, "With all my worldly goods I thee endow." "Well," muttered one of the neighbors, "There goes Sidney's bicycle."

The beautiful girl living in a Miami Beach hotel, got out of bed, put a housecoat on over her sheer nightgown, went to her dressing table and began to comb her hair. In the reflection of her mirror, she noticed the window washer cleaning the windows. She decided that she would give him a thrill so she stood up and stretched her arms above her head, looking at him languidly; but he kept on cleaning the windows. She took off her housecoat, stood in her sheer nightie, walked a couple of feet closer to the window, made a few moves with her hips but no reaction came from the window washer. Finally she took off her nightgown, stood there completely nude, walked right up to the window and glared. The man flung open the window and said, "Wassamatta Lady, ain't you never seen a window washer before?"

"John loves children."

The young couple were canoeing in the middle of the lake when a sudden squall hit.

Terrified at the intensity of the wind and rain, the boy started to pray. "Oh Lord, save us and I'll give up smoking...I'll give up drinking... I'll give up_____."

At this moment the young lady yelled "Don't give up anything else, I think the storms over."

Two little worms were crawling in the garden, one of them stopped and the other crawled right on.

Two sailors were walking down the street in a strange town when a girl stuck her head out of a doorway and shouted: "Come in, fellows and I'll give you something you've never had before." One sailor looked at the other and said: "Run like hell. She's got leprosy."

"Not bad for a fella who can't swim a stroke, eh."

Blonde: "I've been receiving threatening letters in the mail—isn't that against the law?"
Officer: "Why yes, who has been writing them?"
Blonde: "My lover's wife."

The world-renowned German surgeon, Dr. Hans Von Graff was famous for his brilliant appendectomy technique which required only a half-inch incision.

While the doctor was on tour in America, Reggie Gleason, the wealthy playboy, needed his appendix removed. Since his wedding was only a month away, he decided to have Dr. Von Graff perform the operation and avoid the usual scar.

The operation was completed and Reggie came out of the ether to discover, much to his horror, his lower regions a mass of bandages. Calling the nurse, he demanded an explanation of why a half-inch incision should require so many bandages.

"Well," she replied, "there you were in that large amphitheater with a score of prominent surgeons looking on. Doctor Von Graff performed the operation with brilliant ease. His every motion was a thing of beauty. As he finished, he was given a standing ovation. The applause was deafening. The great doctor took many bows, but they refused to stop. Well, Dr. Von Graff got so carried away that for an encore he circumcised you."

A little six year old girl came in and asked, "Mommy can I have babies?" "No, of course not dear." "Alright boys same game."

Inmate: "I have a mad insane desire to crush you in my arms."
Lady Psychiatrist: "Now you're talking sense."

"I told you it was all over between us."

Two old men meet on a corner.
First old man: "Where have you been for the past eight weeks?"
Second old man: "In jail."
First old man: "You in jail? How come?"
Second old man: "Well, about eight weeks ago I was standing on a corner, and this beautiful young girl rushes up with a policeman and says, 'He's the man, officer. He's the one who attacked me.' I tell you, I felt so flattered, I admitted it."

"Send me the bookkeeper," roared the senior partner.

"Listen you," he bellowed when the bookkeeper appeared. "I can't stand for too much more of this. Last year you forged three checks in my name, six months ago you stole thousands of dollars. I discovered you were disclosing our business secrets and several nights ago you took advantage of my daughter. Now, I'm warning you—the next least little thing you do, out you go!"

The difference between amnesia and magnesia is that the person with amnesia doesn't know where he is going.

A beatnik ran a red light, the cop pulled him over and said, "Didn't you see that red light?" The beatnik replied, "Like man I didn't even see the house."

"I still think they don't have to be **that** devoted to us."

Did you hear about the crosseyed seamstress that couldn't mend straight?

Good Times = Wine, women and song.
Hard Times = Beer, pretzels and mama.

Judge: "Did you say this man stole your money out of your stocking?"

Gal: "Yes, your honor."

Judge: "Why didn't you put up a fight?"

Gal: "I didn't know what he was after."

Female Golfer: "I'm troubled with athlete's foot. In fact it keeps me awake at night."
Golf Pro: "Tell the jerk to trim his toe nails."

He met his friend on the street and exclaimed "Call me LUCKY!"

"What happened?" asked his pal.

"I got on the bus this morning and realized that I had forgotten my briefcase at home, so I got off at the next corner. Shortly after, the bus was hit by a truck and two people were killed right where I was sitting."

"Man, you are lucky," retorted the friend.

A week later they met again and the friend was greeted with "Call me LUCKY! LUCKY!"

"What happened now?"

"I missed my Flight 704 to Miami and the plane crashed without any survivors."

"Man, you are LUCKY! LUCKY!" said his friend.

When they next met two weeks later, the friend was hailed with "Call me LUCKY! LUCKY! LUCKY!"

"Now what?"

"Last week I was making love to my girl when the heavy chandelier over her bed fell down and hit me on the rear."

"What's so lucky about that?" asked the pal.

"Shucks man!" he replied, "a minute earlier it would have hit me on the head!"

The fashion world is buzzing with the news that women are going back to the one-piece bathing suit. We're just wondering what piece they'll wear.

It was their honeymoon night and the bride had put on a sheer night-gown and crawled into bed...only to discover that her husband was about to go to sleep on the couch. "George," she called out, "aren't you going to make love to me?" "I can't honey," he replied, "because it's Lent."

"Why that's awful," she exclaimed, bursting into tears. "To whom, and for how long?"

"Alright, once more around and we'll call it a night."

What is the difference between unlawful and illegal?
Unlawful means against the law, illegal is a sick bird.

"He says he'll take it out in trade . . . but he doesn't want beads and trinkets."

A lanky Texan was extremely mad because Texas had just become the second largest state in the Union. So, he made up his mind to move to Alaska. He drove for three days and three nights to get there and finally he came to what looked like the State line. He halted his car and walked up to an elderly farmer whom he figured was a customs inspector.

"Hi, there! How do I become a resident of this here biggest state?" demanded the tall Texan.

The farmer looked him up and down for a moment and grinned. "Waal," he answered, "there are three things you gotta do to get in. First, drink

Continued

down a quart of 110 proof corn lik-
ker without blinkin'. Second, kill a
polar b'ar, and third, make love to
an Eskimo woman.''

''Sounds easy enough,'' said the
Texan. ''Where can I get me a quart
of this here corn liquor.''

''Got one right here,'' replied the
farmer. ''I'll let you have it for
$20.00.

The Texan paid the farmer and then
gulped down the whiskey without
batting an eyelash. ''Now, do you
happen to know where I can find me
a polar bear?''

''Yep,'' answered the farmer, ''thar's
a big female polar b'ar over that way
'bout a mile... lives in a cave by the
ocean.''

The Texan lurched merrily off. About
half-an-hour later he returned with
clothes torn almost off and his face
scratched and bloody. He was smil-
ing happily. ''Now,'' he roared,
''where's that damn Eskimo woman
you want killed?''

JUSTICE OF THE PEACE: ''Wal Clem,
what's this here boy charged with?''
CONSTABLE: ''He's charged with
arson, Sam.''
JUDGE: ''Arson? Gol durn it, there's
been altogether too much arson
around here lately. Now son, you
marry that girl!''

"Then she said, 'The gods will be angry if we do it,' and I said, 'Nonsense' . . ."

The rich old gentleman and his wife were celebrating their 40th wedding anniversary and their three grown sons joined them for dinner. The old man was rather irritated when he discovered that none of the boys had bothered to bring a gift and after the meal, he drew them aside.

"You're all grown men," he said, "and old enough to hear this. Your mother and I have never been legally married."

"What?" gasped one of the sons. "Do you mean to say we're all bastards?"

"Yes," snapped the old man, "and cheap ones, too."

A husband, who wasn't getting along too well with his spouse, threw a big party and invited all his friends.

At the beginning of the evening, everyone sat around talking about various subjects. But as the evening progressed, members of the opposite sex started to couple off and find cozy corners.

Soon, the lights were dimmed, and love and passion dominated the scene. When the husband looked for his wife, he couldn't find her. However, after looking all over the apartment, he stepped into the pantry . . . and there she was, in the passionate embrace of one of his friends. "Your wife and I love each other," his friend told him, "and we want to get married. Can you forgive me for taking her away?"

"Shucks," smiled the husband, "that's what this party was for!"

"Aw c'mon honey, let's go to my apartment instead."

SNAPPY REPARTEE: What you would say if you had another chance.

"My advice to you is to drop out of the Miss America Contest and enter the Mrs. America Contest."

Two prosperous Garment Center manufacturers hired a new model. She was a beautiful girl but she wasn't too bright. The two partners were attracted to the girl, but the interest was not of the paternal nature. "Look," one told his partner, "being that she's so young and pretty, she might be taken advantage of by some fast talking fellow. I think we ought to take it upon ourselves to teach her what's right and what's wrong." "You're right," agreed his partner, "you teach her what's right."

The soldier came home after a year's absence and found his wife sick. He took her to the doctor, who told him confidentially that his wife was pregnant.

"Why that's imposible doctor," said the bewildered soldier. "I've been away for more than a year!"

"Yes, I know," replied the doctor. "We've had cases like this before. We call it grudge pregnancy. You see, someone had it in for you."

"It's alright—we're playing doctor."

A nasty young thing from Peru
Filled up her sweet parts with glue.
　　　She said, with a grin,
　　　"They paid to get in,
Now they'll pay to get out
　　　again, too."

In a small rural school when the teacher stood on tiptoe to reach the top of the blackboard someone snickered behind her. She whirled, indignantly.

"Who did that?"

Little Johnny in the fourth row raised his hand in confession. "I saw your garter, Ma'am."

"Well, for that, you can go straight home now, and don't report back here for a week."

Dutifully, little Johnny obeyed and when the door had closed, the teacher resumed her instruction, reaching even higher on the blackboard. As she did so, another boyish snicker sounded behind her, and again she demanded the name of the wrong-doer.

This time it was small Timmy in the second row.

"Ma'am, I saw both of your garters."

The teacher was outraged. "Go home right this minute! And don't come back for a month."

As she turned again to face the blackboard the now thoroughly shaken teacher dropped her chalk. As she stooped to pick it up, Benny in the first row began gathering his papers, books and pencils together.

"Just what do you think you're doing, Benny?" asked the teacher.

"I'm going home, teacher. I think my school days are over!"

Then there was the beatnik cannibal who ate three squares a day.

Girls who throw themselves at men, actually are taking very careful aim.

"I'm sorry Mr. Jones, but Mother says I can't baby-sit for you anymore."

During the early part of the war, Fred Finster was stationed in England where he became friendly with the local people. One day Fred and an English acquaintance were strolling near a river. On the bank sat a very pretty girl, fishing. Fred called out: "What are you fishing for?" The girl replied, "Men." "How come you are sitting on your bait?" asked Fred. The two men walked along down the river. An hour later the Englishman began chuckling: "That was a very amusing remark you made to that young lady. But how did you know she had worms?"

Happy Husband: I get along great with my Wife.

Hacked Husband: Mine is the demanding type. Buy me, get me, take me. It's murder. For three months she kept hounding me to buy her a Jaguar. "Get a Jaguar, I want a Jaguar." That's all I ever heard from her. Well I finally gave in and bought her a Jaguar, but I was lucky, it ate her.

"Well, congratulations! The night clerk tells me that you two finally got married."

The undertaker sent a telegram to dopey Davis the Taxidermist advising him that his mother-in-law had died and asked whether she should be embalmed, cremated or just buried. He received this reply:

"All three, take no chances."

An Indian sued his wife for divorce. The grounds were:

Injun plant potato—up jump potato.
Injun plant corn—up jump corn.
Injun plant injun — up jump china-man.

"At least **here,** when it's love at first sight, you know what you're getting."

"How on earth do you expect to sell hair tonic? You must be jesting. You haven't any hair at all!"
The salesman snapped back, "So what, I know quite a few guys who sell brassieres!"

Pandemonium: Sex fiend loose in a house of ill repute with a credit card.

A father was shopping in a department store with his small daughter, when the little girl suddenly tugged at his coat sleeve and said, "Daddy, I gotta go."

"In a moment, dear," the father replied.

"No, Daddy, **now!**" the little girl insisted in a voice that could be heard out on the street.

The father's embarrassment was quickly relieved when a saleslady stepped forward and said, "That's all right, sir, I'll take her."

Later, when they were leaving, the father asked his daughter, "Did you thank the nice lady for being so kind?"

"Why should I thank her?" retorted the little girl, as loud as before. "She had to go, too!"

Secretary: "I would like to inform you that I have found a new position."

Boss: "Fine, let's try it!"

Odd-ball son: "Dad, I'm in love with a girl."

Father: "Thank God, you made the right decision."

These days, too many beautiful women are spoiling their attractiveness by using four-letter words—like don't, and can't, and won't.

A legal secretary is any girl over eighteen.

"Nothing important, Dear — Just an old French movie."

Two Englishmen, out for a night on the town, picked up a couple of gals in a dimly lit pub and began touring the town. In one spot, while the girls were occupied in the ladies' room, one of the men whispered to his companion:

"I say, old man, would you mind awfully if we switched dates?"

"Not much," said the other. "But yours seems a decent sort of girl; what's wrong with her?"

"Nothing much," replied the first, "but between the smog and the grog and the fog, I seem to have picked up an aunt of mine."

The high-priced lawyer was sitting in his office when his secretary announced the arrival of a new client: a very sexy doll.

"I wish to divorce my husband," said the doll.

"On what grounds?" the lawyer asked.

"Infidelity," came the reply. "I don't think my husband has been faithful to me."

"What makes you think that?"

"Well," said the dame, "I don't think he's the father of my child."

"Will you be taking over the payments on her fur coat?"

Cabbie: Did someone tell me to stop?

He: Keep going stupid, she wasn't talking to you.

Definition of a Horse Show: A bunch of horses showing their asses to a bunch of horses' asses, showing their asses.

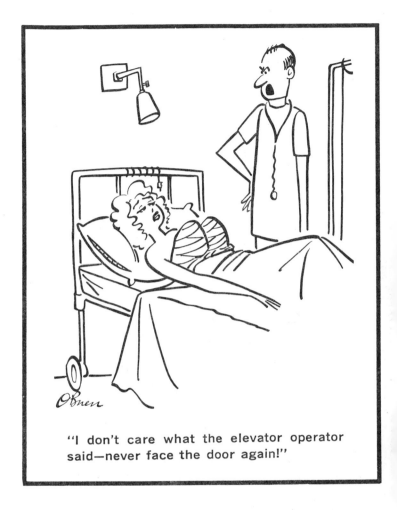

"I don't care what the elevator operator said—never face the door again!"

It was a congenial crowd, the orchestra's music sweet, the multi-colored, dim-lit ballroom full of girls and few men waiting in the stag line.

One of the younger gay blades eyed a lovely for a moment, approached her and bowed. "Miss, may I have the pleasure of the next dance?"

She glanced at the fellow coldly and with a smirk answered, "I'm sorry, Sonny. I don't dance with a child."

"Madam, I beg your pardon," was the lad's quick comeback, "I didn't know you were in that condition."

Little Alfred, much to the horror of his parents, had taken to using profane language to accentuate his vocabulary. Time and time again he promised to give up the bad habit. In desperation his mother threatened to turn him out if he didn't stop. To her dismay he was at it again the very next morning. Putting on a stern expression, she packed his clothes in a bag and sent him out of the house. The little fellow stood on the porch for some time while his mother watched anxiously from the window. Finally she opened the door and put her head out.

"Well," she demanded in mock seriousness, "why don't you leave?"

"Because," replied the lad, tears streaming down his cheeks, "I don't know where the hell to go!"

Trouble with being the best man at a wedding is that you don't get a chance to prove it.

Some guys are born lucky. One man recently received a divorce and got custody of the maid.

Some necklines are so low, they'd make a baby cry.

Never try to keep up with the Joneses; they might be newlyweds.

Ad in the personal column of a large metropolitan daily: "Gentleman who smokes, drinks and carouses wishes to meet lady who smokes, drinks and carouses. Object: smoking, drinking and carousing."

"Your secretary says she won't be at the office today—she has a headache."

Mabel explained to Arthur that she was willing to marry him, but it was equally apparent to Arthur that he hadn't won the approval of Mabel's strong-willed, domineering mother. He asked Mabel why.

"The trouble is," she explained, "my mother thinks you're effeminate."

Arthur thought this over for a moment and then replied:

"Well, sure; compared to her I probably am."

George was asked to give a speech at his lodge meeting and he decided to give a talk on sex in marriage. When he arrived home that night, his wife asked what he'd talked about. George, afraid of her reaction, said he'd spoken about his experiences as a flier.

The next day, George's wife was stopped by a woman whose husband was a lodge member. "That was some speech your husband gave. He must be quite an expert."

"Oh, I wouldn't say that, he's only done it twice. The first time he lost his hat and the second time he got sick to his stomach."

"Did I hear a zipper?"

In the line of duty a census taker approached a farmhouse where he was greeted by a five-year-old boy. "How many in your family?" the census taker asked.

"Four," replied the little boy. "My mama, daddy, sister and me."

"Where's your daddy?"

"Gone fishin', I reckon, 'cause he put on his rubber boots, and it ain't rainin'."

"Well, where's your mother?"

"Well, I guess she's gone out 'cause the catalogue's missin' and she can't read."

"Then where's your sister?" asked the government man.

"I reckon she's down at the barn with the hired hand 'cause there ain't but two things she likes to do —and supper's waitin' on the table!"

"You're Grade A ... I mean, fine ... Miss LaRue."

Two enterprising publishers formed a partnership and over a period of years built up a profitable line of humor diaries. One spring day the elder of the two was lured away from work to join a golf foursome. At lunch time, however, he made a bee-line for the telephone in the locker room and called his office.

"Anything happen this morning, Alex," he asked anxiously.

"Anything happen!" echoed his partner excitedly. "We got the biggest order in our history, that's all."

"Have Miss Tondelaya read it to me right away," cried the senior member.

Miss Tondelaya came to the phone and said brightly, "Here it is, Mr. Kannon. 'Ship immediately forty dozen Daily Dilly. Stop. Eighteen dozen Daily Wit. Stop. Seventy-three dozen Poems for the John. Stop'..."

The angry voice of Mr. Kannon interrupted her recital. "Listen," he screamed to his partner, "you over-sexed idiot, leave that girl alone till she finishes reading the telegram."

Two girls were discussing their psychiatrists:

"My doctor is wonderful. I used to have horrible dreams about men going to bed with me and then offering two dollars for my services. After six months of treatment, that's all changed. I still have the same dream but now they offer me two hundred dollars!"

If you enjoyed this book, you will want the others in this series;

Poems For The John

Jokes For The John

Guest Register For The John

Flushed